Cover Phot
Cover design by Julie M.
On the cover are Trisha McConnell and her dog Lassie

ISBN # 1-891767-02-X

For information contact:
McConnell Publishing, Ltd.
P.O. Box 447
Black Earth, WI 53515
608/767-2435
Fax: 608/767-5802
www.patriciamcconnell.com

Printed in the United States of America

13 14 15

How to be the
LEADER OF THE PACK
...and Have Your Dog Love You For It!

by Patricia B. McConnell, Ph.D.

I know you love your dog. But if you love your dog you will do him no favors by catering to him, continually cooing over him or providing him with no boundaries. Dogs need to feel secure to be truly happy; that means they need to feel secure that you will be the leader, and that they can count on you to take charge. But being the "leader" is often misunderstood. It doesn't mean that you forcibly dominate your dog. Rather, leadership is more of a mental quality, in which you set boundaries without intimidation. Good parents and good teachers know that children need kind and benevolent direction, and good dog trainers know that dogs need the same thing. Like children, all dogs need love, but there's a big difference between being loved and being spoiled. It will do your dog no good to live in a house where she can get anything that she wants by being pushy and demanding. If you are comfortable being a benevolent leader, your dog can relax, and will love you all the more for it.

The following suggestions are an effective and humane way to set boundaries without intimidation and to love your dog without spoiling him. Keep in mind that love is not related to social status, and that most dogs feel happier when they know that they are not responsible for making all the difficult decisions that leaders have to make. Dogs behave as though they prefer knowing that you are in charge, and often seem much happier when they understand that they can count on you to take care of things. Don't think of the steps below as a prescription for being cold or unloving to your dog, but rather as a way of helping your dog learn to get what she wants by being patient and polite, rather than being pushy or demanding.

2

The suggestions below are NOT practices that you must follow every second of every day, no matter how your dog behaves. There are plenty of times I pet one of my dogs when he comes up just to say hello. Who wants a dog if you can't ever pet him just for fun? But you'll do your dog no good if you cater to him like a geisha girl waiting on her master. How strictly you follow the program below depends on your dog's behavior. If your pup seems perfect, you can follow some of these steps some of the time (being aware of them might help keep her that way!) If Ginger gave you a dirty look over her rawhide, then react by following some of these guidelines for leadership over the next couple of hours. If, on the other hand, Spot just bit you, follow the ideas below to the letter for at least a month. (And totally ignore him for the first two days—don't speak to or look at him, even while feeding or letting him out.) Great trainers act like thermostats—easing up when a dog is being polite, becoming a little more "hard to get" when the dog begins to be demanding or too focused on pack hierarchy. No matter how great your dog is, always be careful about catering to him and indirectly forcing him into the lead. It's lonely at the top, so give your dog a break and take over. He'll love you for it, and that's what you want, isn't it?

I. PETTING

I think we pet our dogs for at least two reasons: it feels *really good* to us (and is indeed good for us; it lowers our blood pressure and heart rate), and it's a way to tell our dogs how much we love them. You'd think this would work well, because so many dogs seem to love being petted as much as we love to pet them. When a dog comes up to you, pushes into your space and insists in some way that you pet her, she's not necessarily being sweet, loving or cute. She's *demanding* that you pet her. If you respond, you are teaching your dog that she can insist that you cater to her.

Think about the potential consequences. If your dog can come up and say the equivalent of **"YO! Human! Pet Me...Right NOW!"**, why should she let you take away the pork chop she just stole from the counter?

On the other hand, you can use your dog's desire for attention to motivate her to do what you ask. If she wants to be petted and you'd like to pet her, simply ask her to Sit or Lie Down first. Now she is learning that by being patient and obedient she can still get what she wants. Good Dog!

If you have had any trouble with any type of aggression with your dog, follow the ideas below to the letter. As your dog improves you can modify the instructions a bit, and allow yourself some free pets. (For your sake more than for your dog!) If you have a docile, sweet dog, just keep the following in mind to insure that she isn't getting too demanding.

- Pet only for obedience. (Come, Sit, Lie Down, etc.)

- Keep petting brief—Don't cuddle on the couch eating popcorn, mindlessly petting your dog while you watch a movie. When you stop what happens? She nudges you with her nose, and you, good little subordinate that you are, start petting her again, right?

- If you want to initiate petting, call your dog to you, don't go to her.

If your dog rudely demands petting, either:

- **Body Block** (see below) with your shoulder or elbow, leaning forward with your torso if your dog pushes into your space and then **look away** (fold arms, turn head up and away from the dog).

- and/or, ask for a Sit or a Lie Down, then pet.

2. BODY BLOCKS

Owners who can only control their dogs with leashes have dogs who respect leashes, not owners. A leash can be a useful safety net and occasional training tool, or it can sabotage all your efforts to have your dog listen to you. If you always use your leash to control the movement of your dog, who is in control? Must be the leash. Congratulations, you've just elected a thin strip of nylon as the President of your house.

One of the ways that dogs maintain leadership positions is by controlling the use of *space* of other individuals, rather than by controlling every move the other dog makes. Dogs "herd" each other by simply imposing their body in the direction of travel of other dogs, and so can you. All you need to do is to insert your body in the dog's direction of movement and lean forward slightly. This, for example, is the best way to stop a dog from breaking a Stay: simply watch your dog like a hawk, *and as he starts to get up*, lean your body toward him and raise your arms up and out to effectively block that space. Dogs are very sensitive to this visual signal, so lean backwards a bit when he settles back down or you will be putting too much pressure on him.

Use the same action to block other unwanted moves on his part. For example, what if your dog jumps up on you while you're sitting on the couch? He won't stop doing it if you push your dog away with your hands. I suspect that dogs think hands are simply our pathetic attempt to make up for not having muzzles, and respond by getting mouthy themselves. Additionally, using our paws can make it seem like we are trying to play, because dogs initiate play by using their forepaws. If you get firmer, they either think you *really* want to play or they become defensively aggressive. I have had great luck with a modification of what ethologists call "shoulder slams." The last thing I want you to do is "slam" into your dog, but you can modify this move for effective space management. Pull your hands in toward your chest, and gently push the dog away with your shoulder, or elbow. Using your torso appears to be understood by dogs as a

5

status-related gesture, and is much more effective at stopping dogs from being physically pushy than using your hands. Notice that again you are leaning your body forward *into* the dog, effectively "taking the space" away from him.

Accordingly, don't let your dog move out of his way to cut you off and cause you to redirect your path. That's a clear high-status move in a canid society. If you're walking from point A to point B, and your dog moves in front of you to get in your way, just keep walking forward in tiny steps. Keep your feet on the ground and shuffle along a direct path to where you want to go. Let your dog pay attention to you and where you're going, not vice versa. (Some people advocate insisting that a sleeping or resting dog get up and move out of an owner's path, but this seems awfully harsh. I only walk "through" if it appears that a dog has deliberately gotten in my way.)

You can have a profound effect on how your dog perceives you by imagining an inviolate column of air in front of and around your body. Remember that in our own species, people who command respect also have their "personal space" respected. It's also useful to spend a few weeks paying attention to which way your body is leaning when you work with your dog. For example, if Chester is jumping out of control when it's walk time, do you shift your weight back ever so slightly as he leaps up at you (pretty understandable after all, since Chester might weigh as much as you!), or do you lean forward slightly to "take the space"? This can occur in units of microseconds and millimeters, but start out by exaggerating your actions until they become second nature. *(Caution: if your dog has bitten or seriously threatened you, please don't do this without getting professional help from someone who specializes in treating aggression.)*

3. LOOK AWAYS

If your dog gets "pushy," demanding your attention, simply cross your arms, turn your head upward and to the side away from your dog. If the dog counters by moving to your other side (where your head is directed) turn your head away again. Be sure your chin is tilted up in dismissal, not down as if you're being coy.

If your dog is a status-seeking dog, this is a good thing to do whenever your dog demands that you pet or play with her. Look away *consistently* if your dog has been aggressive toward you—as a matter of fact, you should completely ignore her for several days if she has lunged, snapped or bitten lately.

Looking away is the visual signal sometimes given by high-status dogs toward subordinates and is very very different than the hard, direct stare that some books tell you to give your dog. Be careful of assertive stares to your dog—they are much more confrontational than a dismissive "look away," and might end up putting you at risk.

4. LIE DOWN AND STAY

Teach your dog a good solid Lie Down and Stay. Start with one second stays for the first two days, then quickly work up to longer and longer ones during which your dog gets treats while staying, not when she is released (avoid distractions at this point). After three weeks, most dogs (except energetic juveniles) can handle a half-hour down stay during a quiet time of day when all the rest of the house is quiet. It works best to have them lie down between you and a television; that way you've both found a place to park and the dog is automatically in your line of sight.

Remember that your dog has to learn to stay through all kinds of distractions, and most novice dog trainers expect dogs to stay through difficult distractions much too early in training. So ask for long Down/Stays during quiet times, understanding that your dog will probably get up automatically if you do (so help her by visually signalling Stay before you move). Correct breaks with **Body Blocks**, not by simply repeating "Sit," "Down," and "Stay," over and over again. Pantomime your dog back into place, all the time remaining quiet and calm. If your dog gets up 25 times, then correct her 25 times with the same actions and tone of voice—but do not include anger in your correction. Be very matter-of-fact. Most dogs do best if you work on this silently, except for a quiet "Stay" signal, always given in conjunction with a clear hand signal to help the dog know what you mean.

5. WAIT AT THE DOOR

Alpha dogs have "priority access to limited resources," which means that they get to push out the doorway first to get to something they want. That is probably one of the reasons why so many dog fights occur at doorways over who gets to go out first. This is not different than our species—would you barge into the Pope to get out the door first? If your dog runs into you to get to something she wants, she's not exactly being respectful of you, nor is she being polite and patient. Another reason that some dogs have trouble controlling themselves at the door is a simple lack of frustration tolerance, so teaching dogs to be courteous at the doorway can help your dog to be a polite member of the family.

You can handle the rush to the door in two ways: one is to say "Sit" and "Stay," going through the door first and then releasing the dog to follow you. I think a much better way is to use **Body Blocks** to herd the dog away from the door, then block her again if she tries to go through first without you saying "okay." Avoid using the leash—that is simply an admission to the dog that you have no control. Control the space in front of the dog and you control the dog.

Say you're going out on a walk with your dog. Ginger will probably get to the door first, since dogs all seem to move at the speed of light if they want something. You can't control her if you're behind her, so simply slide your body in between your dog and the door and "herd" her backwards about three or four feet from the door. She'll probably continue to try to get around you to the door, but keep blocking her with your legs (by moving sideways and *forward*) until she pauses. Then move to the door (still facing her) and partially open it. Have your dog on leash if necessary for safety's sake, but do *not* use the leash to control her. Have someone else hold a leash if possible, or tie it to a railing, but don't use the leash to stop her; let your body do it. Most dogs move forward as they see the door open—this is when you should step forward, blocking that space, and again herd your dog away from the door. Once she backs up, step aside from the open door and give her a chance to make her own decision. Always give your dog a choice—don't continually block the opening by draping your body over it—rather, step back a bit so that the dog makes her own choice about whether to wait or to barge through. At the first sign of hesitation, say "okay" and let her out. No need to treat here: what she wanted was out the door, and now she knows how to earn it.

6. FOUR ON THE FLOOR

Dogs interpret an increase in vertical height as an increase in status. Period. End of sentence. It's a *symbol* to us, but a synonym to them. I've seen a sweet puppy-loving female dog turn into a furry chain saw when the owner inadvertently picked a puppy up and held it above the adult female's head. Apparently it looked like the puppy was challenging her for status, and since the pup was seven-weeks old and the adult female had seven years under her collar, she was not impressed. Although the absence of any good research on this has made the subject controversial, my clinical work suggests that dogs who sleep up on the bed are especially impressed with themselves. After all, they are up high and allowed in the royal sleeping quarters. They *must* be important, look where they get to sleep! This is not a problem for most dogs, but you'd be wise to keep status-seeking dogs on the floor—not up on the furniture (especially if you are in the room). If you want to cuddle, *you* get down on the floor, ask for some obedience and then pet. If your dog isn't status-seeking and you've never had any trouble, then go ahead and invite him up to cuddle.

Keeping dogs off the furniture seems impossible to owners whose dogs have slept on the bed for years, but in my experience dogs adapt to this change in routine amazingly fast. An easy way to accomplish this is to leash the dog to the leg of the bed while you sleep. Just take her there each night, pet the ground (give her a doggie bed if you think she'd like it) and say "Go to Bed." You might give her a toy stuffed with food to sweeten the pot. (For safety's sake, be sure that your dog cannot jump over anything while leashed up—that could result in a serious injury.) Never go to a dog who has shown status-related aggression in the past and try to push or pull her off the bed or couch by her collar. This is too dangerous. Rather, call the dog to come off, using positive reinforcement to insure she'll be glad she came.

7. TEACH OFF

Canine pack leaders can warn an individual off of a resource (like a bone or a good sleeping place) with just a warning glance. You can do this too, by teaching your dog to back away from something with just one calm, quiet word. It's a wonderful way to teach your dog to be polite, and it can be a practical way to stop Fido from eating the dinner you dropped or away from your dog-hating relatives.

Start teaching your dog "Off" (or "Leave It"—use whatever word you'd like) with food in a closed hand. Say "Off" immediately before you move the food toward the dog, ending with your fist almost touching the dog's nose. When he tries to eat the treat, keep your hand closed until he moves his head back, even an inch, and stops trying to get the food. When he pauses, even just for a half a second, say "okay" and give him even better food from the other hand. Resist the urge to move the food to him: the message here is "back up" vs. "come forward," so let your dog do the moving while you keep your hand still.

Next, teach your dog to back away from food on the floor when you say "Off," keeping in mind that it's a separate phase of training. (Food "in the hand" is *very* different than food on the floor to a dog, so don't do this if your dog has been seriously aggressive over food, unless you are working one-on-one with a professional.) To teach this next step, move your dog to one side of you, say "Off," and then drop the food onto the floor. Be ready to Body Block him repeatedly until he stops trying for it and pauses. Immediately say "okay," and give him an even better treat from your hand.

Gradually move farther and farther away from the food or toy until you can say "Off" from across the room and have the dog turn and come back to you for his reward.

8. INTEGRATE OBEDIENCE INTO YOUR DAY

Instead of having one long, organized training session each day, your dog will be much better behaved if you integrate obedience into your dog's day, such that it becomes part of her regular routine. It's easy—just ask her to perform some action whenever she wants something (like for you to open the door, to play ball, to get dinner, etc.). Teaching Sit, Down and Stay can easily be accomplished by asking for one or two of those actions as you are playing, walking across the room, going outside, watching TV, etc. The key is to understand that dogs will work to get something that they want—your job is to know what your dog wants at that particular moment. No dog wants food all the time, and no dog wants praise all the time. Just like us, what they want varies from minute to minute. Use this principle so that it works for you rather than against you. Make obedience seem relevant to life, so that your dog begins to learn: "Oh, I see, the way to control my environment and get what I want is to do what she asks."

9. LEADERS ARE IN THE LEAD

Insuring that your dog will heel on cue is an important part of being a leader. *After all, if your dog is in the lead, he's the leader, right?* "Heel" is the perfect way to teach your dog to pay attention to you, and to let you initiate where to go and how fast you get there. Remember, though, you can't teach a good heel simply by forcing your dog to stay beside you. Rather, follow the instructions from books or classes that emphasize positive reinforcement on how to teach heel as a fun game that you and your dog get to play together. Once he knows what *right* is, continue to use positive reinforcement to motivate him to do it correctly. Remember that dog packs don't have anything equivalent to "Heel" (or, from a dog's perspective, "Walk slowly at a boring pace by your owner's left leg, ignoring all interesting things."), so it is up to us to teach our friends what we are talking about, and subsequently to make it worthwhile to continue doing it.

If you have a dog whose main exercise is a neighborhood leash walk, you don't want to keep Fido on "Heel" the entire time. That demands too much focused concentration and not enough relaxation for your dog. But you don't want your dog to haul you around the block either. Solve the problem by only letting your dog direct the activity part of the time. Always begin and end with the dog responding to you rather than vice versa. The first few minutes when you leave the house is the perfect time to insist that she attends to you—after a few minutes (seconds at first) of a good job heeling, let her sniff to her heart's content. Since that's really what she wanted, it's the perfect reward. So, ask for attention as you leave and before you go back into the house, and let your dog have the freedom she earned in between.

10. PLAY

Dogs express many of their status-related issues in play, so you need to be aware of how your play can either promote your dog up the ranks or keep him happy with your leadership. Remember that the pack leader *initiates behavioral change*, so any time that your dog demands something ("Play with me, *now!*", "Pet me, *now*," "Let me out *right now!*") he is promoting himself to camp counselor. You should initiate play sessions, and *you* should be able to stop them with a quiet word. Don't let your dog push you with his nose and demand that you throw the ball. It's not sweet, loving, or cute...it's pushy.

Also, be thoughtful about playing tug of war with your dog. Tug games can be great—not only are they good exercise, they can also be used to teach your dog to regulate his level of emotional arousal, and to "drop it" on cue. However, tug of war can also get you in trouble. If your dog gets overly aroused during tug games, or has a tendancy to bite at the tug toy closer and closer to your hand, you'd be wise to find another way to play. If you do play tug, end the game by taking the toy and putting it away until the next session.

Finally, don't ever "rough and tumble" wrestle play with your dog. I always feel like a witch when I say that, because usually some kind-hearted, dog-loving man's face falls when I do. Make no mistake about it: with some exceptions, this is a guy thing. Male primates engage in "rough and tumble play" so conspicuously that field researchers sometimes use it as an indicator of gender. Indeed, 95% of the people I see in my office who wrestle play with their dogs are men. So I always feel guilty taking away their fun, because there's no doubt that both humans and dogs love it. But, male or female, it teaches dogs to play rough with humans, and it *oh so very often leads to trouble.* Perhaps not with the person who started it, but more likely with the little girl whose parent's are suing you over the "play bite" to their daughter's face. Dogs can get overly aroused in play. And just as fights sometimes break out at ball games in our species, over-arousal can sometimes lead to aggression in dogs.

Instead, play ball, play frisbee, play soccer, teach heel like a game, teach "find it," train tracking, do tricks together, herd sheep, go hunting, have a wonderful, joyful time together, but please, *please* don't wrestle with your dog.

11. A WORD ABOUT FOOD

There is no reason not to use food to initiate a new command with your dog. The problem some people have is that they *always* give the dog food for compliance—and soon have a dog who *only* performs if you have food. You can easily prevent this, by simply using food intermittently and focusing on using other reinforcements to insure your dog is glad to be obedient. Use intermittent reinforcement in two ways: vary what the dog gets for obeying (food, praise, play, get to pee!, belly rubs, etc.) and don't always give the dog something. Intermittent reinforcement always gets the best results. After all, how many quarters would you put in a slot machine before you got something back? Now compare that to how many you'd put into a Coke machine if you didn't get your pop the first time. If you always expect a reward, your behavior ceases quickly if you don't get something every time; but if you never know when the pay off will come, you persist, just like you want your dog to do!

12. ALPHA ROLL-OVER...DON'T DO IT!!!

Be careful about doing the often-advised "alpha roll-over" in which owners are told to flip their dogs over onto their backs and stand over them, growling and staring. This is supposed to be a good way to exert your dominance, because it is similar to behavior seen in a wolf pack. But dogs aren't wolves, and even if they were, there's a difference between discipline and an all-out fight over status. Wolves discipline puppies by gently biting their muzzles—a behavior that my attorney and I suggest you avoid!   Dogs indeed can start fights by grabbing another dog by the scruff, but people don't win dog fights, so don't start one.

Besides, remember that in wolf packs and dog-dog interactions, lower status animal roll over on their backs *voluntarily*—they aren't forced into it. Throwing your dog over onto her back and then threatening her will only elicit fear or fear-related aggression, and that's not being a benevolent leader, that's being a bully.

Following these guidelines will provide your dog with the security he or she wants and needs. Don't think of these as punishments, but rather as boundaries that clarify and structure your relationship. Your dogs will love you for it. Bless their furry little hearts.

Other books and booklets by
Patricia B. McConnell, Ph.D.

For The Love of a Dog
Understanding Emotions in You and Your Best Friend

The Other End of the Leash
Why We Do What We Do Around Dogs

The Cautious Canine
How to Help Dogs Conquer Their Fears

I'll Be Home Soon!
How to Prevent and Treat Separation Anxiety

The Fastidious Feline
How to Prevent and Treat Litter Box Problems

Books with other authors

Family Friendly Dog Training: A Six Week Program for You and Your Dog
Patricia B. McConnell and Aimee M. Moore

Feisty Fido
Help for the Leash Aggressive Dog
Patricia B. McConnell and Karen B. London

Feeling Outnumbered?
How to Manage and Enjoy Your Multi-Dog Household
Karen B. London and Patricia B. McConnell

Way to Go!
How to Housetrain a Dog of Any Age
Karen B. London and Patricia B. McConnell

Puppy Primer
Brenda Scidmore and Patricia B. McConnell

**Visit our Website for more information about
ordering books (and VIDEOS!)
www.patriciamcconnell.com**